Wild Women Talk Back

Wild Women Talk Back

Audacious Advice for the Bedroom, Boardroom, and Beyond

Autumn Stephens

CONARI PRESS

First published in 2004 by Conari Press,
an imprint of Red Wheel/Weiser, LLC
York Beach, ME

With offices at:
368 Congress Street
Boston, MA 02210
www.redwheelweiser.com

Library of Congress Cataloging-in-Publication Data

Wild women talk back : audacious advice for the bedroom, boardroom, and beyond / Autumn Stephens.

   p. cm.

Includes index.

ISBN 1-57324-967-X

1. Women—Quotations. I. Stephens, Autumn, 1956-

PN6084.W6W55 2004

305.4—dc22   2004008975

Book design by Maxine Ressler
Typeset in Memphis, Kaufmann, and Fournier
Printed in Canada
TCP

11 10 09 08 07 06 05 04
8   7   6   5   4   3   2   1

CONTENTS

*P*lease give me some good advice in your next letter. I promise not to follow it.

—*Edna St. Vincent Millay*

One-size-fits-all usually *doesn't*—a rule that applies equally to pantyhose and pertinent advice. And why, indeed, should it, given the teeming multitude of female forms, the panoply of human psyches? Of course, if you find it impossible to squeeze 60 percent of your body mass into a miniscule bit of fragile, "flesh"-colored nylon tubing, it is probable that you will lead an interesting and useful life nonetheless. Queen Elizabeth I, after all, never heard of Queen Size. Madam Curie didn't know from Control Top. Isadora Duncan managed to turn modern dance on its head without ever purchasing a single garment labeled "Nude, Size B."

Likewise, we can all survive just fine without any more one-size-fits-all advice of the "horizontal stripes make the midriff appear massive," and "never let a strange man have his way with you" ilk. As for the first statement, wouldn't that mondo midriff actually be an asset in fending off amorous attentions? And as for the second, as feminist author Robin Morgan once noted, "*All* men are strange." Zero population growth is all well and good—but do you really want it to start with you?

This, however, is not your mother's advice. Ten to one, Mama never mentioned that some *women* are only interested in one thing. (To wit, the actress Valerie Perrine, quoted herein: "I don't care what a man thinks of me as long as I get what I want from him—which is usually sex.") Unlike comic Roseanne Barr, your mother probably also failed to point out the positive side of PMS: "I think of it as the only time of the month when I can be myself." And unless your maternal progenitor was the essayist Amy Krouse Rosenthal, she almost certainly never urged you to polish off that second slab of pie, cooing that "Nobody's last words have ever been, 'I wish I had eaten more rice cakes.'"

From sex to motherhood (not, incidentally, unrelated phenomena), from physical appearance to self-esteem, from coping with a career to attaining wisdom, the dozens of Wild Women in this collection offer their own brash brand of counsel and commentary on themes common to most women's lives. Unlike those pesky pantyhose, the following tips and quips will do absolutely nothing to flatten your tummy. But surely they will lift your spirits.

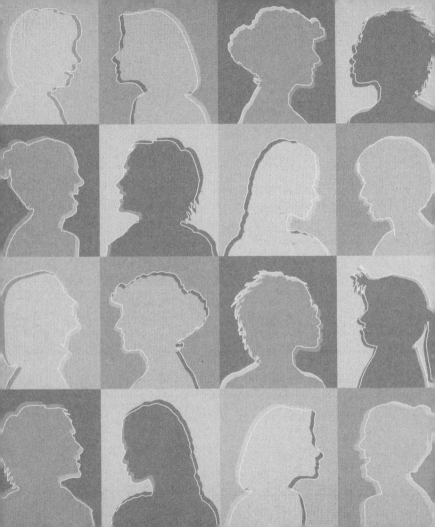

CHAPTER ONE

—◆—

*Self-Esteem:
On Being the
Bee's Knees*

—◆—

*A*long with a few million other Baby-Girl Boomers, I was fortunate enough to grow up in an era when it wasn't a crime for a young woman to call attention to herself. Scholastic achievement, in particular, was an okay way for a girl to get her props. Yet outright showing off, at least in my household of origin, remained taboo. I still squirm to recall my mother's reaction when, during the course of a Girl Scout meeting which she was leading, I fell histrionically to the floor and lay there flopping like a landed flounder. I no longer recall the reason for this bit of childish buffoonery (I was perhaps ten or eleven at the time), or the reaction of my cookie-selling compatriots. But my mother's disapproving face and stern admonition reverberate through my memory cells to this day. "Why, that's just like saying, 'Look at me! Look at me!'" she scolded.

Okay, so I adore my (loving, funny, shockingly smart) mother; I really do. And in the early sixties, with the sweeping cultural changes of that decade scarcely spawned, no doubt her reaction to a crassly attention-seeking daughter was the norm. Yet why, I now wonder, in a world where the wind can so easily be knocked out of a woman's sails (whether deliberately and cruelly, or just by the sheer impersonal weight of accumulated experience), would we strive to diet down our daughters' egos? Wouldn't it make more sense to shore them up to the size of J. Lo's celebrated booty, so that they'd still retain a little buoyancy, a modicum of *oomph!*, despite the inevitable deflationary effects of life?

Happily, the parents of the outspoken Wild Women in this section seem to have been spectacularly enlightened . . . or, perhaps, merely spectacularly unsuccessful at inculcating the creed of mouse-like behavior in their daughters. For amplification of your own sassy Attitude—or perhaps just your own Amusement—read on.

*I*f you always do what interests you,
at least one person is pleased.

—*Katherine Hepburn, icon of American theater*

*I*t's very expensive to be me.

—*Anna Nicole Smith, well-off widow*

I thank God I am endowed with
such qualities that if I were turned out of the
Realm in my petticoat I were able to live in
any place in Christendom.

—*Elizabeth I, Queen of England*

I will not be vanquished.

—*Rose Kennedy, matriarch*

*V*inegar he poured on me all his life; I am
well marinated; how can I be honey now?

—*Tillie Olsen, political activist/*
award-winning short story writer

I belong to that group of people who
move the piano by themselves.

—*Eleanor Robson Belmont, nurse/playwright/*
founder of Metropolitan Opera Guild

*D*id you hear what I said?
It was very profound.

— *(Dr.) Laura Schlessinger,*
sharp-tongued radio shrink

*I*n southern Spain, they made me eat
a bull's testicles. They were really garlicky,
which I don't like. I prefer to take a
bull by the horns . . .

—*Padma Lakshmi, actress*

*T*here's a very good reason why women live longer than men. They deserve it.

—*Estelle Ramey, endocrinologist*

*S*o long has the myth of feminine inferiority prevailed that women themselves find it hard to believe that their own sex was once and for a very long time the superior and dominant sex.

—*Elizabeth Gould Davis, liberated librarian*

*I*t is not easy to find happiness in ourselves,
and it is not possible to find it elsewhere.

—*Agnes Repplier, essayist*

*W*hen I fight, there is usually
a funeral and it isn't mine.

—*Henrietta Green, fearless financier*
of the nineteenth century

*Y*ou show people what you're willing to
fight for when you fight your friends.

—*Hillary Clinton, lawyer, politician,*
and veteran presidential spouse

*T*he question is not whether we
will die, but how we will live.

—*Joan Borysenko, mind-body healer*

A woman who is willing to be herself
and pursue her own potential runs not so
much the risk of loneliness as the challenge
of exposure to more interesting men—
and people in general.

—*Lorraine Hansberry*, Raisin in the Sun *playwright*

*M*y master had power and law
on his side; I had a determined will.
There is might in each.

—*Harriet Ann Jacobs, author of the autobiographical*
Incidents in the Life of a Slave Woman

*W*omen are natural guerrillas.
Scheming, we nestle into the enemy's bed,
avoiding open warfare, watching the
options, playing the odds.

—*Sally Kempton, journalist turned yoga guru*

*W*e are not interested in the possibilities of defeat. They do not exist.

—*Victoria, the velvet-gloved Queen of England*

*N*o one really listens to anyone else, and if you try it for a while you'll see why.

—*Mignon McLaughlin, aphorist*

*R*emember, if you write anything nasty about me, I'll come round and blow up your toilet.

—*Courtney Love, macho musician*

*P*assivity and quietism
are invitations to war.

—*Dorothy Thompson, the first American journalist
banned from Nazi Germany*

*Y*ou have to be taught to be second class;
you're not born that way.

—*Lena Horne, entertainer/civil rights activist*

*I*t is, indeed, a trial to maintain the virtue
of humility when one can't help being right.

—*Judith Martin, aka the venerable Miss Manners*

*I*t requires philosophy and heroism
to rise above the opinion of the wise men of
all nations and races.

—*Elizabeth Cady Stanton, suffragist leader*

*T*he first and worst of all frauds is to
cheat one's self. All sin is easy after that.

—*Pearl Bailey, entertainer of* Hello Dolly *fame*

I came out of the womb a diva. All it
means is you know your worth as a woman.

—*Cindi Lauper, proud pop singer*

*W*hy is there so much pressure to spend
Independence Day with other people?

—*Betsy Salkind, comedienne*

*G*et your cut throat off my knife.

—*Diane di Prima, beat bard*

I am my own Universe, I my own Professor.

—*Sylvia Ashton-Warner, New Zealand writer*

I'm so popular it's scary sometimes.
I suppose I'm just everybody's type.

—*Catherine Deneuve, femme fatale of many a French film*

*S*ome feminists feel that a woman should never be wrong. We have a right to be wrong.

—*Alice Childress, actress/playwright/director*

*P*rudent people are very happy; 'tis an exceeding fine thing, that's certain, but I was born without it, and shall retain to my day of Death the Humour of saying what I think.

—*Lady Mary Wortley Montagu, world traveler and letter writer of the eighteenth century*

*I*n spite of honest efforts to annihilate my *I-ity*, or merge it in what the world doubtless considers my better half, I still find myself a self-subsisting and alas! self-seeking *me*.

—*Jane Welsh Carlyle, one-half of very literary nineteenth-century marriage*

*D*o what you are afraid to do.

—*Mary Emerson, the righteous aunt of Ralph Waldo*

*N*othing is so pleasant as to display your worldly wisdom in epigram and dissertation, but it is a trifle tedious to hear another person display theirs.

—*Ouida, luxury-loving novelist of nineteenth-century England*

*I*f you send up a weather vane or
put your thumb up in the air every time you
want to do something different, to find out
what people are going to think about it,
you're going to limit yourself. That's a very
strange way to live.

—*Jessye Norman, opera singer*

*B*y whom?

—*Dorothy Parker, toast of the Algonquin Table,
on being told that she was "outspoken"*

A real diva would never scream at her guests to get out. She would ask her assistants to make the guests get out. This is one of the rules of divadom.

—*Donatella Versace, an expert in the ways of her kind*

*T*he world is wide, and I would not waste my life in friction when it could be turned into momentum.

—*Frances Willard, nineteenth-century social reformer, on learning to ride a bicycle*

CHAPTER TWO

Love 'n' Lust 'n' Stuff

*B*rilliant, reclusive Emily Dickinson—at first blush, a truly improbable tease—slyly observed that her refusal to marry only piqued her suitor's desire. "Don't you know that 'No' is the wildest word we consign to language?" gloated the seductive (verbally, anyway) poet. Not, I hasten to add, that Dickinson's aloofness constituted a calculated strategy á la the Rules Girls. The truth is, the woman was so thoroughly averse to togetherness, romantic or otherwise, that she would sometimes converse only with those who agreed to remain in an adjoining room, or hidden behind a screen. Let's just say it must have seemed like a real milestone (and possibly proof of advanced metaphysical skills) to merely slip your arm around elusive Emily.

At the opposite end of the Love 'n' Lust continuum, let us place Joan Crawford, the sizzling screen queen, who might be said to have posted a metaphorical "We're Open!" sign on her boudoir door. As La Crawford explained, she found sex vital to maintaining her glowing complexion. One can easily imagine that the same tonic contributed to the peaches-and-cream visage of voluptuous Mae West, who intimated (though not, as it happens, entirely accurately) that she never married because "I would have had to give up my hobby." But how, then, to account for the unblemished beauty of Sharon Stone, who once bitterly opined that "Women might be able to fake orgasms. But men can fake whole relationships"? Obviously, one woman's hot affair is another's arid hell.

From clogged-pore commentary to hormonally turbo-charged talk, you're about to encounter an abundance of provocative positions. Just don't forget that a girl can obtain excellent skin care products at the drugstore, too.

*I*f it has tires or testicles,
you're going to have trouble with it.

—*Linda Furney, U.S. politician*

*P*ersonally, I like sex and I don't care
what a man thinks of me as long as I get what
I want from him—which is usually sex.

—*Valerie Perrine, film attraction*

I don't want to say that I want a man
to like me for my mind, because that's going to
sound like I think I'm Albert Einstein.
But I would like someone who doesn't accuse
me of making up words like "segue."

—*Mariah Carey, singer*

I never married because I would have
had to give up my favorite hobby.

—*Mae West, self-styled sex goddess*

*C*linton lied. A man might forget where he parks or where he lives, but he never forgets oral sex, no matter how bad it is.

—*Barbara Bush, former first lady*

*I*f there is anything disagreeable going on, men are sure to get out of it.

—*Jane Austen, the perennially popular novelist*

I have no patience with women who measure and weigh their love like a country doctor dispensing capsules. If a man is worth loving at all, he is worth loving generously, even recklessly.

—*Marie Dressler, character actress of the thirties*

I really detest movies like
Indecent Proposal and *Pretty Woman*
because they send a message to women that
sleeping with a rich man is the ultimate
goal—and really, that's such a small part of it.

—*Laura Kightlinger, comic*

I knew that the men I married were very attractive to the opposite sex: the twenty marriages they had between them proves that, if nothing else does.

—*Ava Gardner, thrice-wed actress*

*I*f men knew what women laughed about, they would never sleep with us.

—*Erica Jong, women's writer*

*B*ig doesn't necessarily mean better.
Sunflowers aren't better than violets.

—*Edna Ferber, Pulitzer Prize-winning novelist*

*I*mpotent!

—*Louise Colet, French journalist,*
describing a disappointing tryst in her diary

*L*ove is the difficult realization that something other than oneself is real.

—*Iris Murdoch, bright light of Brit lit*

*I*t was not cold.
There was a fire in the studio.

—*Pauline Bonaparte, Napoleon's black sheep sister,*
explaining why she was comfortable modeling minus clothes

*E*verybody should practice safe sex.
'Cause nobody wants to be doing it
and put an eye out.

—*Emmy Gay, "Fusion Art" entertainer*

*M*y attitude toward men who mess around
is simple: If you find 'em, kill 'em.

—*Loretta Lynn, vengeful vocalist*

*T*oo many cooks spoil the brothel.

—*Polly Adler, madam*

*W*omen complain about sex more than men. Their gripes fall into two major categories: (1) Not enough. (2) Too much.

—*Ann Landers, advice columnist*

*S*aying that men talk about baseball
in order to avoid talking about their feelings
is the same as saying that women
talk about their feelings in order to avoid
talking about baseball.

—*Deborah Tannen, a top name in twentieth-century linguistics*

*I*f you have enough fantasies, you're ready,
in the event that something happens.

—*Sheila Ballantyne, American author*

*W*omen might be able to fake orgasms.
But men can fake whole relationships.

—*Sharon Stone, contemporary actress*

*L*orena Bobbit said her husband
didn't satisfy her sexually. Well, honey,
if you thought it was bad before . . .

—*Brett Butler, the so-called Southern Lenny Bruce*

I'd rather pay a young man's fare to California than tell an old man the distance.

—*Jackie "Moms" Mabley, generation-spanning jokesmith*

*L*ove never dies of starvation,
but often of indigestion.

—*Ninon de Lenclos, considered the crème de la crème
among courtesans in seventeenth-century France*

*B*etter an old man's darling
than a young man's slave.

—*Alberta Martin, the "Oldest Living Confederate Widow,"
who married a man sixty years her senior*

*F*or women the best aphrodisiacs
are words. The G-spot is in the ears. He who
looks for it below there is wasting his time.

—*Isabel Allende, acclaimed Chilean-American novelist*

*S*ome men know that a light touch
of the tongue, running from a woman's toes
to her ears, lingering in the softest way
possible in between, given often enough
and sincerely enough, would add
immeasurably to world peace.

—*Marianne Williamson, spiritual superstar*

*A*morality, or a more complicated morality,
aims at the ultimate loyalty and overlooks
the immediate and literal one.

—*Anais Nin, taboo-trashing diarist*

*T*o talk about adults without talking
about their sex drives is like talking about a
window without glass.

—*Grace Metalious,* Peyton Place *novelist*

*B*eing in therapy is great. I spend
an hour just talking about myself. It's kinda
like being the guy on a date.

—*Caroline Rhea, television talk show host*

*T*he infantile needs of adult men
for women have been sentimentalized and
romanticized long enough as "love"; it is time
to recognize them as arrested development.

—*Adrienne Rich, renowned radical poet*

I don't see much of Alfred any more
since he got so interested in sex.

—*Clara Kinsey, spouse of the controversial sexologist*

*W*ith lovers like men, who needs torturers?

—*Susanne Kappeler, social sciences professor/student of pornography*

*N*o one ever expects a great lay
to pay all the bills.

—*Jean Harlow, Hollywood hottie of the 1930s*

*T*here were three of us in the marriage,
so it was a bit crowded.

—*Diana,* Princess of Wales

*Y*ou don't have to be anti-man
to be pro-woman.

—*Jane Galvin Lewis, founder of
the National Black Feminist Organization*

*E*stimated from a wife's experience,
the average man spends fully one-quarter
of his life in looking for his shoes.

—*Helen Rowland, garrulous gender critic*

*I*f a man sends me flowers, I always look
to see if a diamond bracelet is hidden
among the blossoms. If there isn't one,
I don't see the point of flowers.

—*Hedy Lamarr, leading lady/inventor*

*T*he women's movement hasn't
changed my sex life. It wouldn't dare.

—*Zsa Zsa Gabor, much-married celebrity*

I thought I told you to wait in the car.

—*Tallulah Bankhead, the flamboyant actress,*
on running into an old flame

I have more sex appeal
on the tip of my nose than many women
in their entire bodies.

—*Audrey Hepburn, the epitome of elfin elegance*

I wear a T-shirt that says
"The family tree stops here."

—*Suzanne Westenhoefer, trés gay comic*

I'm like the Statue of Liberty.
No one wants to pay for the upkeep, but
everybody wants to say they've been there.

—*Priscilla Davis, Texas socialite*

*T*he most common cause of impotence
is marriage to other women.

—*Cynthia Heimel, dish-and-tell essayist*

*B*efore accepting a marriage proposal,
take a good look at his father.
If he's still handsome, witty, and has all
his teeth ... marry him instead.

—*Diane Jordan, humorist*

*O*pposites attract—and then aggravate.

—*Joy Browne, radio psychologist*

*I*f your sexual fantasies were truly of interest
to others they would no longer be fantasies.

—*Fran Lebowitz, the flippest lip in the East*

*M*arriage is a matter of give and take,
but so far I haven't been able to find anybody
who'll take what I have to give.

—*Cass Daley, actress*

*T*he most important thing in a relationship
between a man and a woman is that
one of them must be good at taking orders.

—*Linda Festa, widely quoted wit*

*Y*ou [men] are not our protectors.... If you
were, who would there be to protect us from?

—*Mary Edwards Walker, physician/prisoner of war
of the Confederate Army*

*Y*ou can always spot a well-informed man—
his views are the same as yours.

—*Ilka Chase, actress/memoirist*

*T*here are times not to flirt:
when you're sick, when you're with
children, and when you're
on the witness stand.

—*Joyce Jillson, astrologer*

*S*ex:

That pathetic shortcut suggested by nature the supreme joker as a remedy for our loneliness, that ephemeral communion which we persuade ourselves to be of the spirit when it is in fact only of the body— durable not even in memory!

—*Vita Sackville-West,*
amorously adventurous Bloomsbury author

*W*omen have one great advantage
over men. It is commonly thought that if
they marry they have done enough, and need
career no further. If a man marries, on the
other hand, public opinion is all against him
if he takes this view.

—*Rose Macaulay, named Dame
of the British Empire for her polished prose*

*T*alking from morning to night about sex has helped my skiing.

—*Dr. Ruth Westheimer, sexologist, describing the similarities between two popular pastimes*

*D*r. Ruth says we women should tell our lovers how to make love to us. My boyfriend goes nuts if I tell him how to drive!

—*Pam Stone, equestrienne comedienne*

*M*ountains appear more lofty the nearer
they are approached, but great men
resemble them not at all in this particular.

—*Marguerite Power, the Countess of Blessington,*
and a noted novelist

*A*h, the sex thing.
I'm glad that part of my life is over.

—*Greta Garbo, the enigmatic Swedish*
actress, at the age of sixty-nine

I still miss my ex-husband,
but my aim is improving.

—*Debbie Marsh, pistol owner*

*T*he only thing I miss about sex
is the cigarette afterward.

—*Florence King, acerbic author*

I'm deeply disappointed
by my sexual interest in men.

—*Diamanda Galas, non-mainstream musician*

... *B*asically, I've dodged that
marriage bullet ... I like the jewelry
part of getting married, but I can buy
my own damn rings, too.

—*Queen Latifah, rap royalty*

*T*hese are very confusing times.
For the first time in history a woman is
expected to combine intelligence with a sharp
hairdo, a raised consciousness with high
heels, and an open, non-sexist relationship
with a tan guy who has a great bod.

—*Lynda Barry, cartoonist*

*F*alling in love is
no way of getting to know someone.

—*Sheila Sullivan, psychologist*

I don't sit around thinking that I'd like to have another husband; only another man would make me think that way.

—*Lauren Bacall, actress and erstwhile Bogart bride*

*T*he advantage of love at first sight is that it delays a second sight.

—*Natalie Clifford Barney, literary salon hostess*

I'd rather kiss pigs than my husband.

—*Sue Parkinson, founder of a California swine sanctuary*

*O*ne hour of right-down love
Is worth an age of dully living on.

—*Aphra Behn, England's first female professional writer*

I don't have a love life. I have a like life.

—*Lorrie Moore, author lauded for literary irony*

*F*or me, on a scale of one to ten,
romance comes about eighth, after chess
but before politics and football.

—*Alice Thomas Ellis, creator of cookbooks and novels*

*M*en are always ready to respect
anything that bores them.

—*Marilyn Monroe, blonde bombshell*

I have always found husbands much more satisfying after marriage than during.

—*Peggy Guggenheim, patron of the arts*

*I*n the United States of America, there are over 25,000 sex phone lines for men. You know how many there are for women? Just three. Apparently for women, if we want someone to talk dirty and nasty to us, we'll just go to work.

—*Felicia Michaels, comedienne*

*B*efore they're plumbers or writers
or taxi drivers or unemployed or journalists,
men are men. Whether heterosexual or
homosexual. The only difference is that some
of them remind you of it as soon as you
meet them, and others wait for a little while.

—*Marguerite Duras, noted novelist/screenwriter*
of the French "New Wave"

In my opinion, a man is a Man
if he is good at sex.

—*Julie Burchill, British journalist*

Don't wreck a sublime chocolate experience
by feeling guilty. Chocolate isn't like
premarital sex. It will not make you pregnant.
And it always feels good.

—*Lora Brody, author of*
Growing Up on the Chocolate Diet

*A*bsence does not make the heart grow
fonder, but it sure heats up the blood.

—*Elizabeth Ashley, Broadway star of the swinging sixties*

*D*on't put an absurdly high value on him.
Think of the millions of other girls
doing without him, yet able to bear it!

—*Orfea Sybil, unsung wit*

I need sex for a clear complexion,
but I'd rather do it for love.

—*Joan Crawford, diehard diva*

*T*he ultimate test of a relationship
is to disagree but to hold hands.

—*Alexandra Penney, women's magazine writer/editor*

*G*iving a man space is like
giving a dog a computer: the chances are
he will not use it wisely.

—*Bette-Jane Raphael, satirist*

*W*hite men make up only 8 percent
of the world population.
I find that an encouraging fact.

—*Deborah Rhode, Stanford law professor*

*M*en who consistently leave
the toilet seat up secretly want women
to get up to go to the bathroom in the
middle of the night and fall in.

—*Rita Rudner, the sovereign of stand-up whimsy*

... *T*he great divide is still with us, the awful split, the Us and Them. Like a rubber band tautened to the snapping point, the polarization of the sexes continues, because we lack the courage to face our likenesses and admit to our real need.

—*Colette Dowling, best known for the* Cinderella Complex

*I*t is no longer obligatory upon a woman
to give herself to one man to save herself from
being torn to pieces by the rest.

—*Jane Cunningham Croly, founder of the
nineteenth-century woman's club movement*

*T*he fantasy that we are overwhelmed
by Rhett Butler should be traded in for
one in which we seize state power
and re-educate him.

—*Sandra Lee Bartky, philosophy professor*

*T*ake the wife.

—*Edwina Currie, British health minister, advising male travelers how to avoid contracting AIDS abroad*

*P*art of the reason that men seem so much less loving than women is that men's behavior is measured with a feminine ruler.

—*Francesca M. Cancian, sociologist*

*T*o call a man an animal is to flatter him;
he's a machine. . . . It's often said
that men use women. Use them for what?
Surely not pleasure.

—*Valerie Solanas, separatist and sex worker,*
in her infamous SCUM Manifesto

*Y*ou don't have a man, you need spaghetti.

—*Oprah Winfrey, the Big O herself*

*T*he Bible contains six admonishments to homosexuals and 362 admonishments to heterosexuals. That doesn't mean that God doesn't love heterosexuals. It's just that they need more supervision.

—*Lynn Lavner, women's musician*

*S*cratch most feminists and underneath
there is a woman who longs to be a
sex object. The difference is that is not
all she wants to be.

—*Betty Rollin, television correspondent/breast cancer expert*

*M*aybe I've been married a few
too many times. I love a good party, but I have
recently realized that I can actually just
throw a party and not get married.

—*Whoopi Goldberg*

I haven't had sex in eight months.
To be honest, I now prefer to go bowling.

—*Lil' Kim, rapper*

*T*he problem with people who have no vices
is that generally you can be pretty sure they're
going to have some pretty annoying virtues.

—*Elizabeth Taylor, public figure*

I should be groaning over the sins
I have committed, but I can only sigh
for what I have lost.

—*Heloise, nun during the Middle Ages*
whose lover was castrated for copulating with her

I am ashamed of confessing
that I have nothing to confess.

—*Fanny Burney, big-deal eighteenth-century novelist*

*V*irtuous people are simply
those who have . . . not been tempted
sufficiently.

—*Isadora Duncan, interpretive dance pioneer*

I can't be a wife.
I'm not that sort of person.

—*Sarah Brightman, singer*

*N*o pressure, no diamonds.

—*Mary Case, indie film screenwriter*

CHAPTER THREE

Mirror, Mirror, on the Wall: On Being a Babe (or Not)

*S*ome blame the media. Others point their fingers at overbearing parents or capitalism or some vast secret conspiracy to keep women down. But in my humble opinion, this insane obsession with physical perfection is all Mother Nature's fault. You know what I mean. The gyrations at the gym. The calorie counting and carb bashing. The plucking and shaving. The highlights and hennas. The sheer amount of potential college tuition poured into clothes and cosmetics. Oh, and that weird white cream that some beauticians, I swear to God, refer to as "spackle" because it fills in those little creases around the eyes that people who are alive *do* tend to get.

For the last couple hundred years, you see, Mama N. has no doubt been intending to recalibrate our compulsion to, well, perpetuate the species. But you know how it is being a mother—just one thing after another and then boom! all of a sudden the darn thing is overperpetuated. So here we are in the age of space travel and video games, still smearing our lips with berry juice and trying to feign a youthful vibrancy that potential mates will interpret as a delightful sign of fertility. *Very colorful lips! Must perpetuate now!* Well, that's *my* excuse for engaging in shopping therapy, anyway. (As Dolly Parton said, "People think I'm as shallow and superficial as I look, and it's a surprise when they find out, sure enough, I am.") Still, I admire the friend of mine, a musician, who recently quit makeup cold turkey. It seems that she looked around at the members of her choral group one night and realized—*really* realized— that none of the tenors or basses had spent a single second trying to make their faces look more fecund.

But hey, relax, will you? From world-class lovelies to lipstick lesbians to the-hell-with-it ex-hippies, not one of the ladies quoted herein wants to quell your quest to look cute. Nor, for that matter, will you be counseled to schedule a colonic, liposuction your cranium, or nibble on arsenic (as did fashionably pale—and paler, and paler, and dead—ladies of the nineteenth century). There is a distinct possibility, however, that you will find yourself inspired to work on your inner self with the same fervor that you devote to your exterior. For, as the following chapter implies, the finest feature that any woman can possess is self-confidence.

I think I'm a very pretty girl. I'm never
going to pretend to think otherwise.

—*Milla Jovovich, model*

I look older than everybody else
because I haven't had any plastic surgery yet.

—*Cybill Shepard, an actress of the unreconstructed school*

*T*o dance confident in fringe panties when
you're five-four with cellulite is a great thing.

—*Drew Barrymore, butt-kicking* Angel

*W*hy is it considered seductive for women to wear beautiful clothes? Wouldn't it make more sense to wear something so ugly that a guy couldn't wait to take it off you?

—*Flash Rosenberg, multimedia humorist*

*W*hen a photographer shoots a celebrity, they must be taking photos of our inner selves, because I'm always shocked by the way I look . . . I'm way hotter in my own mind.

—*Pamela Anderson, bosomy* Baywatch *alum*

I ask people why they have deer heads
on their walls. They always say, "Because it's
such a beautiful animal." There you go!
I think my mother is attractive,
but I have photographs of her.

—*Ellen Degeneres, uncloseted comic*

*M*ost lesbians are thought to be ugly,
neurotic and self-destructive and I just am not.

—*Rita Mae Brown, writer/babe-magnet*

*W*hoever said money can't buy happiness
simply didn't know where to go shopping.

—*Bo Derek, pinup of perfect 10 fame*

I'm not overweight.
I'm just nine inches too short.

—*Shelly Winters, substantial screen presence*

*W*hen you're not blond and thin,
you come up with a personality real quick.

—*Kathy Najimy, actress*

*N*obody's last words have ever been,
"I wish I had eaten more rice cakes."

—*Amy Krause Rosenthal, nationally noted essayist*

*O*h, never mind the fashion.
When one has a style of one's own, it is
always twenty times better.

—*Margaret Oliphant, prolific Scottish prose writer*

I think women are more interesting in their
forties. . . . They don't have to be hip
and cool anymore, which is a godsend.

—*Jodie Foster, fortyish film star*

I was very sophisticated when I was
seventeen. When I was fourteen,
I was the oldest I ever was. . . . I've been
getting younger ever since.

—*Shirley Temple Black, child actress/adult diplomat*

*I*nside every older woman is a young girl
wondering what the hell happened.

— *Cora Harvey Armstrong, gospel singer*

*B*y the time I'd grown up, I naturally
supposed that I'd grown up.

—*Eve Babitz, all-around artsy type*
(famously photographed playing chess in the nude)

*A*nother belief of mine:
that everyone else my age is an adult,
whereas I am merely in disguise.

— *Margaret Atwood, Canadian fiction writer*

I do wish I could tell you my age but it is impossible. It keeps changing all the time.

—*Greer Garson, American actress*

*H*ow do they know
how big my boomerang is?

— *Margaret, Princess of England, on learning that she was to be presented with a "quilted boomerang cover" in Australia*

I love thongs. The day they were invented,
sunshine broke through the clouds.

— *Sandra Bullock, actress*

I'm a big woman. I need big hair.

—*Aretha Franklin, soul singer*

I much prefer being a man.
Women have to spend so much time pulling
themselves together,
and their shoes kill your feet.

— *Shirley Booth,*
Academy Award winner of 1953

I put this coat on layaway.
It was this brown suede thing and I thought it
was fabulous, the ultimate. I had it for about
two days when our house got robbed,
and it was stolen. . . . If you see me sobbing in
a movie, I'm thinking about that.

— *Julia Roberts, boffo box office draw*

I'm not small, I'm space-efficient.

— *Rachael Leigh Cook, Generation Y actress*

*T*hey don't know if [women in the military]
can fight or kill. I think we can. All the general
has to do is walk over to the women
and say, "You see the enemy over there? They
say you look fat in those uniforms."

— *Elayne Boosler, first lady of one-liners*

I went shopping last week looking for
feminine protection. I looked at all the
products and I decided on a .38 revolver.

—*Karen Ripley, stand-up comic*

*G*uys are lucky because they get to grow
mustaches. I wish I could. It's like having a
little pet for your face.

—*Anita Wise, humor writer*

I'd rather wear black in August
than do one sit-up.

—*Joy Behar, talk show host*

*I*f the shoe fits, it's too expensive.

—*Adrienne Gusoff, professional goofball*

*A*lways serve too much hot fudge sauce on
hot fudge sundaes. It makes people
overjoyed, and puts them in your debt.

—*Judith Olney, a chef uncowed by calories*

I keep my campaign promises,
but I never promised to wear stockings.

—*Ella T. Grasso, former governor of Connecticut*

I'm nothing to look at, so the only thing I can
do is dress better than anyone else.

—*Wallis Simpson, the clotheshorse for whom
Edward VII abdicated the throne*

*N*ever "just run out for a few minutes"
without looking your best.
This is not vanity—it's self-liking.

—*Estee Lauder, makeup maven*

*H*ow long can you be cute?

—*Goldie Hawn, aging actress*

*T*he heck with the natural look. Where would Marilyn Monroe be if she'd clung to the hair color God gave her? We'd have a movie called *Gentlemen Prefer Mousy Brown Hair.*

—*Adair Lara, essayist*

*Y*ou have to do everything you can to make your butt stand out. But for me, I think I have enough to sit on, so it's fine.

—*Shakira, pop singer*

*I*f I had been around when Rubens was painting, I would have been revered as a fabulous model. Kate Moss . . . would have been the paintbrush.

—*Dawn French, British sitcom star*

I'm the kind of woman who, when she walks into a party, all the other women leave the room . . .

—*Lara Flynn Boyle, cinematic bad girl*

*T*he only weights I lift are my dogs.

—*Olivia Newton-John, singer/celebrity cancer survivor*

*T*here's times when I just have to quit
thinking . . . and the only way I can quit
thinking is by shopping.

—*Tammy Faye Bakker, a Christian
of the capitalist persuasion*

A woman's dress should be like
a barbed-wire fence: serving its purpose
without obstructing the view.

—*Sophia Loren, screen siren*

A woman reading *Playboy* feels a little
like a Jew reading a Nazi manual.

—*Gloria Steinem, a seminal figure in modern feminism*

*W*omen dress alike all over the world:
they dress to be annoying to other women.

—*Elsa Schiaparelli, fashion designer*

*C*lothes and courage have
much to do with each other.

—*Sara Jeannette Duncan, the first female journalist
employed full-time by the* Toronto Globe

*W*omen are all female
impersonators to some degree.

—*Susan Brownmiller, feminist historian*

A dress makes no sense unless it inspires men to want to take it off you.

—*Françoise Sagan, sexy French fiction writer*

I try to be as unsexy as possible.

—*Dusty Springfield, singer*

*Y*ou can have anything you want in life if you dress for it.

—*Edith Head, hallowed costume designer*

*P*eople think I'm as shallow and superficial as I look, and it's a surprise when they find out, sure enough, I am.

—*Dolly Parton, curvaceous country-and-western artist*

*I*t is not possible for a man to be elegant without a touch of femininity.

—*Vivienne Westwood, punk-positive fashion designer*

*P*eople who keep stiff upper lips find
that it's damn hard to smile.

—*Judith Guest, novelist*

I see my body as an instrument,
rather than an ornament.

—*Alanis Morissette, singer of the woman-scorned school*

*T*here are an awful lot of skinny
people in the cemetery.

—*Beverly Sills, opera singer*

CHAPTER FOUR

Working Women (Oh, Like There Are Any Other Kind)

*T*wo years, two apartments, and two boyfriends after I was divorced, I had a shocking realization: I was still employed in *the same job* that I had entered as a newlywed. As so often happens, I had taken the position as a stopgap measure, with the plan of eventually acquiring work more in line with my values and goals. How startling it was to realize that the job that had seemed so tangential to my *real* life had turned out to be the most consistent factor in it.

While you, dear lady, are almost certainly a less capricious and more self-aware individual than I was as a young adult, it is likely that we have at least this in common: work is the mainstay of our existence. Whether we toil nine to five (or, more likely these days, eight to six) just to keep body and soul together, or whether we're lucky enough to labor with love, we'll probably spend most days of our adult lives engaged in work of one sort or another. (On the bright side, grownups can have ice cream whenever they want, even in the middle of the night if they feel like it.)

This chapter, then, is for everyone. For those who haven't yet discovered a gratifying way to earn their daily bread. (Prime minister, anyone? How about porn writer?) For those who are curious to know how other women get through the work day. (With pleasure, with passion, with heaping infusions of caffeine). For those who harbor dire suspicions about the flip side of success (Ready for speculation about your sexual preference, Ms. Overachiever)? And for those who are at work right this minute, bored out of their everloving bazoos.

A career is erotically sexual,
it's my real passion. A career is like always
having a mistress on the side.

—*Raquel Welch, sixties sex symbol*

*O*nce you look down the barrel of a 9mm gun,
starting a business is a piece of cake.

—*Aliza Sherman, pioneering Internet entrepreneur*

*M*y, I'm a loud lady. No crooner, I.

—*Judy Garland, actress/singer/Minnelli mom*

I get so tired listening to one million dollars here, one million dollars there, it's so petty.

—*Imelda Marcos, former first lady of the Philippines*

*T*he easiest kind of relationship is with ten thousand people, the hardest is with one.

—*Joan Baez, protest singer*

*R*adical simply means
"grasping things at the root."

—*Angela Davis, FBI fugitive turned academician*

*O*ne must be frank to be relevant.

—*Corazon Aquino, former president of the Philippines*

*I*f they don't call you a lesbian, you're
probably not accomplishing anything.

—*Cheris Kramarae and Paula Treichler,*
the cheeky coauthors of the Feminist Dictionary

*I*f I'd been a housemaid I'd have been
the best in Australia—I couldn't help it.
It's got to be perfection for me.

—*Nellie Melba, coloratura*

*B*ehind every successful woman . . .
is a substantial amount of coffee.

—*Stephanie Piro, cartoonist*

*I*f one is going to change things, one has to make a fuss and catch the eye of the world.

—*Elizabeth Janeway, best-known for the* Powers of the Weak

*I*f the bird *does* like its cage, and *does* like its sugar, and will not leave it, why keep the door so very carefully shut?

—*Olive Schreiner, South African feminist author*

*N*ever do anything yourself
that others can do for you.

—*Agatha Christie, author of many a masterful mystery*

*N*o more tears now;
I will think about revenge.

—*Mary, Queen of Scots*

I should like to be a horse.

—*Elizabeth II, Queen of England*

*I*f it's a good idea . . . go ahead
and do it. It is much easier to apologize
than it is to get permission.

—*Grace Murray Hopper, computer programming pioneer*

*H*ow we spend our days is,
of course, how we spend our lives.

—*Annie Dillard, Pulitzer Prize winner*

*B*eing the best divorce lawyer in New York
is like being the best devil in hell.

—*Judith Regan, Big Apple book editor*

I don't intend for this to take on
a political tone. I'm just here for the drugs.

—*Nancy Reagan, former first lady of the*
United States, misspeaking ever so slightly

I learned to make my mind large,
as the universe is large, so that there
is room for paradoxes.

—Maxine Hong Kingston,
chronicler of Chinese-American angst

*M*y personal hobbies are reading,
listening to music, and silence.

—Edith Sitwell, England's publicity-loving poet

I never felt I left the stage.

—*Helen Gahagan Douglas,*
actress, opera singer, and politician

*T*here are two reasons
why I am successful in show business
and I am standing on both of them.

—*Betty Grable, whose glam gams were*
insured for one million dollars

*I*t doesn't matter if you win
or lose, until you lose.

—*Angie Papadakis, advertising executive*

*I*f you dance, you dance because you have to.
Every dancer hurts, you know.

—*Katherine Dunham, dance troupe founder*

I've had so many rebirths, I should
come with my own midwife by now.

—*Cher, an entertainer for the ages*

*O*nly a fool would try to compress a
hundred centuries into a hundred pages of
hazardous conclusions. We proceed.

—*Ariel Durant, coauthor of the comprehensive* Story of Civilisation

*W*hen you perform . . . you are for
minutes heroic. This is power. This is glory
on earth. And this is yours nightly.

—*Agnes DeMille, choreographer*

I'm not funny. What I am is brave.

—*Lucille Ball, of* I Love Lucy *fame*

*I*t's a nightmare when I travel. I show up
at the airport with a suitcase full of legs and
I'm always over the limit.

—*Heather Mills, distributor of used artificial limbs*

*D*on't Pee On My Leg
and Tell Me It's Raining

—*Judge Judy Sheindlein, courtroom TV star,*
who thusly titled her second tome

*T*he one important thing I have
learned over the years is the difference
between taking one's work seriously and
taking one's self seriously. The first is
imperative and the second is disastrous.

—*Margot Fonteyn, prima ballerina*

I'm anal retentive. I'm a workaholic. I have
insomnia. And I'm a control freak. That's why
I'm not married. Who could stand me?

—*Madonna, chameleonesque celebrity, in 1991*

I don't mind how much my ministers talk—as long as they do what I say.

—*Margaret Thatcher,*
former prime minister of England

*Y*ou have to admit that most women who have done something with their lives have been disliked by almost everyone.

—*Françoise Gilot, painter pal of Picasso*

I'm comfortable with money and
it's comfortable with me.

—*Diana Ross, soul singer*

I was raised almost entirely on turnips and
potatoes, but I think that the turnips had more
to do with the effect than the potatoes.

—*Marlene Dietrich, actress noted for her androgynous mystique*

*T*he state you need to write is that state
that others are paying large sums to get rid of.

—*Shirley Hazzard, Australian novelist*

*A*gatha Christie has given more
pleasure in bed than any other woman.

—*Nancy Banks Smith, TV critic*

*I*t's never too late to be
what you might have been.

—*George Eliot, the scandalously unwed scribe*

I am sorry to see you in this predicament,
but had you fought like a man you would not
now have to die like a dog.

—*Anne Bonney, eighteenth-century pirate,
to "Calico Jack" Rackham, her colleague/lover,
on the eve of his hanging*

*M*ost men have learned to enjoy
loving a doer rather than a dodo.

—*Helen Gurley Brown, steno pool type turned
swinging* Cosmopolitan *editor-in-chief*

*A*fter me there are no more jazz singers.

—*Betty Carter, self-confident songstress*

*M*en for the sake of getting a
living forget to live.

—*Margaret Fuller, iconoclastic nineteenth-century intellectual*

*W*hat I know about money I learned
the hard way—by having had it.

—*Margaret Halsey, British satirist*

*H*aving money is rather like
being a blond. It is more fun but not vital.

—*Mary Quant, mini-skirt inventor*

I wouldn't say I invented tacky,
but I definitely brought it
to its present high popularity.

—*Bette Midler, eccentric entertainer*

*E*ven in my blunders, I overachieve.

—*Cathy Guisewaite, in her comic strip,* Cathy

*W*hat could I do? I wasn't young,
I wasn't pretty, it was necessary to
find other weapons.

—*Dominique Aury, who penned the sexy*
Story of O *as an aphrodisiac for her man*

*D*on't talk to me about rules, dear.
Wherever I stay I make the goddamn rules.

—*Maria Callas, temperamental La Scala star*

*T*here's only one thing I never did and
wish I had done: climbed over a fence.

—*Mary, Queen of England*

I have something to prove, as long as I know
there's something that needs improvement,
and you know that every time I move, I make
a woman's movement."

—*Ani Difranco, contemporary singer*

[*How*] men despise women
who have real power.

—*Eleanor Roosevelt, famous first lady*

I travel a lot, and every day I'm
in a different hotel. For some reason, people
mistake me for the maid. The other day
this guy says, "You can come into my room
and do your job now!" So I went in there and
told him some jokes.

—*Bertice Berry, African-American TV personality*

I have no regrets. I wouldn't have lived my life the way I did if I was going to worry about what people were going to say.

—*Ingrid Bergman, adulterous actress*

*W*e don't know who we are until we see what we can do.

—*Martha Grimes, mystery writer*

I was brought up in a clergyman's
household, so I am a first-class liar.

—*Dame Sybil Thorndike, thespian*

*E*verybody's an artist. Everybody's God.
It's just that they're inhibited.

—*Yoko Ono, out-there vocalist/Beatle wife*

I'm not afraid that the book
will be controversial, I'm afraid it will
not be controversial.

—*Flannery O'Connor, Southern author*

*I*f you want to stand out,
don't be different, be outstanding.

—*Meredith West, professor of psychology and biology*

I thought I could change the world.
It took me a hundred years to figure out I can't
change the world. I can only change Bessie.
And honey, that ain't easy either.

—*Annie Elizabeth ("Bessie") Delaney, African-American
dental surgeon whose liberated life spanned 104 years*

*M*y business is sex, drugs, rock and roll.

—*Whitney Houston, headliner*

I haven't been everywhere yet,
but it's on my list.

—*Susan Sontag, culture critic*

I always chose sophisticated parts because
you can't really be interesting as a young girl
or outstanding as an ingenue.

—*Norma Shearer, who made a big splash in silent films*

"*G*ood gracious, is Jeanette MacDonald
going to take off her clothes—*again?*"

—Jeanette MacDonald, fretting over
audience reaction to her frequent on-screen nudity

*S*uccessful competitors want to win.
Head cases want to win at all costs.

—Nancy Lopez, featured in the Ladies
Professional Golf Association hall of fame

*A*ll I really want to be is boring.
When people talk about me, I'd like them
to say, "Carol's basically a short Bill Bradley."
Or, "Carol's kind of like Al Gore in a skirt."

—*Carol Mosley-Braun,*
the first black woman to serve as a U.S. Senator

I can never remember being afraid of an audience. If the audience could do better, they'd be up here on stage and I'd be out there watching them.

—*Ethel Merman, Broadway musical marvel*

I'm a priest, not a priestess. "Priestess" implies mumbo jumbo and all sorts of pagan goings-on. [But] they can call us all the names in the world—it's better than being invisible.

—*Carter Heyward, Episcopal priest*

*T*iming and arrogance are decisive
factors in the successful use of talent.

—*Marya Mannes, literary light*

*A*s long as the plots keep arriving
from outer space, I'll go on with my virgins.

—*Barbara Cartland, belle of the bodice-rippers ball*

*A*ll things are possible until
they are proved impossible—and even the
impossible may only be so, as of now.

—*Pearl Buck, internationally noted novelist*

*I*t's not how fast you get there,
but how long you stay.

—*Patty Berg, golf pro*

*V*ice president—it has such a nice ring to it!

—*Geraldine Ferraro, first woman nominated for U.S. vice president*

*A*erodynamically, the bumble bee shouldn't be able to fly, but the bumble bee doesn't know it so it goes on flying anyway.

—*Mary Kay Ash, cosmetics tycoon*

I've gotten more VIPs into tights and
codpieces than anyone in this country.

> —*Carol Adelman, business consultant*
> *who uses Shakespeare as a teaching tool*

*T*he secret of my success is that no woman
has ever been jealous of me.

> —*Elsa Maxwell, hot party hostess*

A lot of young girls have looked
to their career paths and have said they'd
like to be chief. There's been a change in the
limits people see.

—*Wilma Pearl Mankiller, Cherokee chief*

I'm living proof that if you
get enough degrees, you'll grow up to
run a dog restaurant.

—*Taimi Gorman, the well-educated owner
of a canine cuisine joint*

*T*here is a time for work.
And a time for love.
That leaves no other time.

—*Coco Chanel, the much-loved designer*

I was 32 when I started cooking;
up until then, I just ate.

—*Julia Child, the cheeriest chef in history*

*M*y father dealt in stocks and
shares and my mother also had a lot of
time on her hands.

—*Hermione Gingold, character actress*

I know [my corn plants] intimately,
and I find it a great pleasure to know them.

—*Barbara McClintock, Nobel Prize-winning scientist*

*E*xperience isn't interesting till
it begins to repeat itself—in fact, till it
does that, it hardly is experience.

—*Elizabeth Bowen, Irish writer*

*F*or a long time I thought I wanted to
be a nun. Then I realized that what I really
wanted to be was a lesbian.

—*Mabel Maney, who has the gay
Nancy Drew literary genre all to herself*

I'd probably be famous now
if I wasn't such a good waitress.

—*Jane Siberry, erstwhile hash-slinger,*
now an internationally acclaimed musician

*W*rite to amuse? What an appalling
suggestion! I write to make
people anxious and miserable and to
worsen their indigestion.

—*Wendy Cope, contemporary poet*

I don't advise anyone to take
[painting] up as a business proposition,
unless they really have talent,
and are crippled so as to deprive them
of physical labor.

—*Grandma Moses, geriatric primitivist*

*T*hink bigger!
Be a millionaire, don't marry one.

—*Nell Merlino, cofounder of*
Take Your Daughter to Work Day

*I*n my own experience,
anyone can paint if he doesn't have to.

—*Beatrice Lillie, lippy Canadian actress of yore*

A sobering thought: what if,
at this very moment,
I *am* living up to my full potential?

—*Jane Wagner, award-winning author of*
The Search for Signs of Intelligent Life in the Universe

CHAPTER FIVE

—◆—

Child Rearing
and
House Keeping

—◆—

*M*otherhood doesn't begin with milk and cookies, but with an ordeal more on the morphine-and-Scotch order. Ejecting your standard-issue seven-pound baby requires at least the machismo of a Hemingway hero (an equivalent facility with expletives is also helpful). And while the rest of child rearing seldom requires such extreme physical fortitude, giving birth is *nada, nada, y pues nada* compared to the emotional stamina required to actually raise said child for the next eighteen or so years.

Nor, having reproduced or otherwise acquired offspring, are women allowed to laze around on their laurels, performing simple tasks such as keeping their progeny (a) alive and (b) out of jail. No, the Modern Mama now labors (metaphorically or otherwise) under the rubric of Having It All. Why *not* have a family and also circumnavigate the globe by hang glider, convert the entire continent to organic farming, campaign for president of the world? Oh, yes, and why *not* spit shine your house and produce a trio of wholesome yet kid-pleasing meals every blessed day of your life, while you're at it? Well, no reason at all, except that it's damn near impossible, that's all, at least if you're the kind of parent who's inclined not only to acquire children, but also to actually spend time with them subsequently.

Of course, most of us are fundamentally gaga about the fruit of our loins, despite the all-encompassing chaos they introduce into our lives. (They're especially dear when they're asleep.) In general, I believe, we're also fond of our homes. But there isn't a woman alive who'll tell you that the domestic goddess gig is a breeze. For a reminder of what it's like to toil in the trenches of tradition—and a little sisterly support for those of us who refuse to accept "short order cook" as a synonym for "mother"—read on.

*W*hen I had my baby,
I screamed and screamed. And that
was just during conception.

—*Joan Rivers, unrivaled reparteeist*

*T*he flip side of the maternal
instinct is the killer instinct.

—*Melissa Soalt, aka "Dr. Ruthless,"*
women's self-defense instructor

*M*om and Pop were just a couple of
kids when they got married. He was eighteen,
she was sixteen and I was three.

—*Billie Holiday, the legendary jazz singer*

*T*ranquilizers work only if you
follow the advice on the bottle—keep
away from children.

—*Phyllis Diller, the famously frazzled comedienne*

... *I*f people tell you your mother is not
prime minister anymore, you just
turn around and say, "So what? How often has
your mother been prime minister?"

—*Benazir Bhutto, former prime minister of Pakistan,
recounting her rather esoteric maternal advice*

I'm a virgin and I brought up all
my children to be the same.

—*Shirley Bassey, vocalist*

A child be within you forever unborn!

—*Irish curse, clearly conceived by a woman*

*W*hy do grandparents and grandchildren
get along so well?
They have the same enemy: the mother.

—*Claudette Colbert, screwball comedy star*

*T*he emotional, sexual, and psychological stereotyping of females begins when the doctor says, "It's a girl."

—*Shirley Chisholm, the first African-American woman elected to the U.S. Congress*

*T*hink of stretch marks as pregnancy service stripes.

—*Joyce Armor, who penned* Letters from a Pregnant Coward

*W*rinkles are hereditary.
People get them from their children.

—*Doris Day, Hollywood's rare "wholesome" type*

*A*bove the titles of wife and mother, which,
although dear, are transitory
and accidental, there is the title human being,
which precedes and outranks every other.

—*Mary Ashton Livermore, nineteenth-century social reformer*

*S*ome of us still get all weepy when we think about the Gaia Hypothesis, the idea that earth is a big furry goddess-creature who resembles everybody's mom in that she knows what's best for us. But if you look at the historical record—Krakatoa, Mt. Vesuvius, Hurricane Charley, poison ivy, and so forth down the ages—you have to ask yourself: Whose side is she on, anyway?

—Barbara Ehrenreich, antisocial analyst

*M*others are a biological necessity;
fathers a social invention.

—*Margaret Mead, anthropologist*

*T*o nourish children and raise
them against odds is in any time, any place,
more valuable than to fix bolts in cars or
design nuclear weapons.

—*Marilyn French, a permanent fixture of feminist literature*

I dream of giving birth to a child
who will ask: "Mother, what was war?"

—*Eve Merriam, poet*

I'm as good a mother as the next repressed,
obsessive-compulsive paranoiac.

—*Anne Lamott, bestselling single mom*

*S*ome people were raised by wolves.
I was raised by drag queens.

—*Margaret Cho, comic monologist*

I don't have a bank account, because I
don't know my mother's maiden name.

—*Paula Poundstone, gag girl*

*F*amily is just accident.... They don't mean to get on your nerves. They don't even mean to be your family, they just are.

—*Marsha Norman, Pulitzer Prize-winning playwright*

*S*hould a woman give birth after thirty-five? Thirty-five is enough kids for anybody.

—*Gracie Allen, George Burns' goofy sidekick*

I love my family, my children . . .
but inside myself is a place where I live all
alone and that's where you renew your
springs that never dry up.

—*Pearl S. Buck, who won a Nobel Prize for her prose*

I never thought you should be
rewarded for the greatest privilege of life.

—*Mary Roper Coker, Mother of the Year 1958*

. . . *M*y opinion is that the future good or bad
conduct of a child depends on its mother.

—*Letizia Ramolino Buonaparte,*
who gave birth to a boy named Napoleon

*M*otherhood is a wonderful thing—
what a pity to waste it on children.

—*Judith Pugh, artist and author*

I don't even butter my bread;
I consider that cooking.

> —*Katherine Cebrian,*
> *San Francisco socialite*

I would rather lie on a sofa
than sweep beneath it.

> —*Shirley Conran,*
> *ʰish journalist/designer*

*I*f you want to get rid of stinking odors
in the kitchen, stop cooking.

—*Erma Bombeck, broad humorist*

I'd like to marry a nice
domesticated homosexual with a fetish
for wiping down formica and different
vacuum-cleaner attachments.

—*Jenny Éclair, top banana*

*W*omen used to have time to
make mince pie and had to fake orgasms.
Now we can manage the orgasms,
but we have to fake the mince pie. And
they call this progress.

—*Allison Pearson, British journalist*

*T*aking responsibility for yourself
and your happiness gives great freedom
to children. . . . Seeing a parent fully
embrace life gives the child permission to
do the same, just as seeing a parent
suffer indicates to the child that suffering
is what life is about.

—*Robin Norwood, self-help sage*

*B*y and large, mothers and housewives are
the only workers who do not have regular time
off. They are the great vacationless class.

—*Anne Morrow Lindbergh, writer*

*A*n ounce of sequins can
be worth a pound of home cooking.

—*Marilyn vos Savant, syndicated brain*

*E*veryone said it was really moist.

—*Kristi Yamaguchi, World Championship ice skater,
on roasting her first Thanksgiving turkey*

CHAPTER SIX

More Womanly Wisdom

*F*rom day one, gender shapes our experience of the world, and how we are experienced *by* the world. On a spiritual plane (or, for that matter, on a crashing plane), the distinction between male and female may be irrelevant. But in our daily lives, nothing is more crucial than whether we queue up outside the ladies' room or stride straight into the (strangely vacant!) men's.

Just imagine how it would feel—and how much time it would save—to jump out of bed in the morning, do nothing more than run a comb through your hair, and consider yourself presentable to your fellow human beings. Or to engage in a romantic encounter without eighteen years of child rearing as a potential consequence. (Now that's a *real* timesaver for you.) Or to loudly appraise the sexual attractiveness of passersby—a recurring revenge fantasy of mine back in the years when I often wished to be invisible. (That is to say, the years before I hit middle age and discovered that my wish had, not altogether agreeably, come true). In other words, there's a good reason that we sometimes feel that we have more in common with some random gal just ahead of us in the grocery store line than we do with our own boyfriends and husbands. We do.

The issues addressed in this final chapter vary wildly—from how to cope with a crying jag, for example, to when you shouldn't fib to where to find God. Yet the common experience of womanhood—with all its profound plusses, with all its maddening minuses—informs each commentator's remarks. Listen, and you'll hear incitement to rebel against sexism. You'll hear the cry for reform of every stripe. And, I sincerely hope, you'll hear the refrain that is the *sine qua non* of Wild Womanism: thinking—and speaking—for oneself.

*F*emaleness, as any
doctor will tell you, is savage.

—*Marion Hilliard, Ontario-born ob/gyn*

*O*nly dead fish
swim with the stream all the time.

—*Linda Ellerbee, TV commentator*

*W*omen complain about premenstrual syndrome, but I think of it as the only time of the month when I can be myself.

—*Roseanne Barr, born-to-be-edgy actress*

*I*f I ever did manage to find a law to live by, I would break it.

—*Exene Cervenka, punk rocker*

*W*omen might start a rumor but not a war.

—*Marga Gomez, star of*
the San Francisco comedy scene

*W*omen are not inherently
passive or peaceful. We're not inherently
anything but human.

—*Robin Morgan, founder of*
the first international women's think tank

*I*f you want something in life, you have to
go out and get it, because it's just not going to
come over and kiss you on your lips.

—*Renee Scroggins, poverty-born musician*

*I*f you want a high performance
woman, I can go from zero to b*tch in
less than two seconds.

—*Krystal Ann Kraus, zinger flinger*

I think we can agree racial prejudice is stupid. Because if you spend time with someone from another race and really get to know them, you can find other reasons to hate them.

—*Bernadette Luckett, scribe of the small screen*

*R*ules are for people who don't know how to get around them.

—*Tori Harrison, college basketball coach*

*Y*ou can cry, but don't let it stop you. Don't cry in one spot— cry as you continue to move.

—*Kina, pop singer of the mono-moniker sort*

*F*etters of gold are still fetters, and the softest lining can never make them so easy as liberty.

—*Mary Astell, eighteenth-century English philosopher*

*R*evolution begins with
the self, in the self.

—*Toni Cade Bambara, writer*

*T*he single most impressive fact about
the attempt by American women to
obtain the right to vote is how long it took.

—*Alice Rossi, past president of the
American Sociological Association*

*T*here was a time when patience
ceased to be a virtue. It was long ago.

—*Charlotte Perkins Gilman, economist,*
author, and celebrated hater of housework

*T*hat you can't fight City Hall
is a rumor being circulated by City Hall.

—*Audre Lord, poet*

*I*f one cannot invent a really convincing lie,
it is often better to stick to the truth.

—*Angela Thirkell, English author*

*T*he beaten track
does not lead to new pastures.

—*Indira Ghandi, prime minister of India*

*Y*ou are a victim of the rules you live by.

—*Jenny Holzer, avant-garde artist*

*P*raying is like a rocking chair—
it'll give you something to do,
but it won't get you anywhere.

—*Gypsy Rose Lee, enlightened ecdysiast*

*W*hen I die, I hope to go
to Heaven, wherever the hell that is.

—*Ayn Rand, ruggedly individualistic author*

I want all hellions to quit
puffing that hell fume in God's clean air.

—*Carry Nation, a very vocal social reformer*

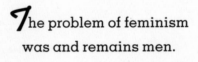

*T*he problem of feminism
was and remains men.

—*Naomi Segal, researcher in the realm of gender*

*T*he world has never yet seen a truly great
and virtuous nation because in the
degradation of woman the very fountains of
life are poisoned at their source.

—*Lucretia Mott, eighteenth-century abolitionist and suffragist*

*I*t's a good thing to have all the props
pulled out from under us occasionally.
It gives us some sense of what is rock under
our feet, and what is sand.

—*Madeleine L'Engle, Newberry Medal-winning novelist*

I tend to treat my emotions like unpleasant relatives—a long-distance call once or twice a year is more than enough. If I got in touch with them, they might come to stay.

—*Molly Ivins, political pundit*

*T*he fullness of life is in the hazards of life.

—*Edith Hamilton, classics scholar*

*J*ust because you're miserable
doesn't mean you can't enjoy your life.

—*Annette Goodheart, Ph.D., practitioner of
"therapeutic laughter therapy"*

*I*n spite of the cost
of living, it's still popular.

—*Kathleen Norris, author of an
astonishing eighty-two novels*

*W*hen men are oppressed, it's tragedy;
when women are oppressed, it's tradition.

—*Bernadette Mosala, South African educator*

*L*ook, I don't even
agree with myself at times.

—*Jeanne Kirkpatrick, U.S. diplomat*

*A*ll sins are attempts to fill voids.

—*Simone Weil, anorectic anarchist*

*B*efore you criticize someone, you should
walk a mile in their shoes. That way,
when you criticize them, you are a mile away
from them, and you have their shoes.

—*Frieda Norris, doyenne of drollery*

*H*ope is the denial of reality.

—*Margaret Weis, sci-fi specialist*

*I*t is brave to be involved
To be not fearful to be unresolved.

—*Gwendolyn Brooks, poet*

*N*o.

—*Amy Carter, erstwhile U.S. president's daughter,
when asked if she had any message for American youth*

*N*o matter how cynical you get,
it's impossible to keep up.

—*Lily Tomlin, grande dame of good humor*

*T*he dying process begins the minute we are born, but it accelerates during dinner parties.

—*Carol Matthau, actress/wife of the legendary Walter*

*S*uperior people never make long visits.

—*Marianne Moore, poet*

*N*ever, never trust anyone who asks for white wine. It means they're phonies.

—*Bette Davis, Big Movie Star*

I got an A in philosophy because I
proved my professor didn't exist.

—*Judy Tenuta, stand-up sensation*

I make mistakes;
I'll be the second to admit it.

—*Jean Kerr, genre-spanning scriptwriter*

*W*e have too many high-
sounding words, and too few actions
that correspond with them.

—*Abigail Adams, first lady No. 2*

*T*hey say that God is everywhere,
and yet we always think of
Him as somewhat of a recluse.

—*Emily Dickinson, poet*

*Y*ou come into the world alone and you
go out of the world alone, yet it seems
to me you are more alone while living than
even going and coming.

—*Emily Carr, crusty Canadian artist*

*L*ife is better than death, I believe,
if only because it is less boring,
and because it has fresh peaches in it.

—*Alice Walker, acclaimed author of*
The Color Purple, *and so on*

INDEX OF WILD WOMEN